JOHANN SEBASTIAN B.

CONCERTO

for Violin, Strings and Basso Continuo

E major / E-Dur

BWV 1042

Edited by / Herausgegeben von
Max Strub

Piano reduction by / Klavierauszug von
Wilhelm Weismann

EDITION PETERS

LONDON · FRANKFURT/M. · LEIPZIG · NEW YORK

Concerto II

Joh. Seb. Bach
(1685–1750)

*) Die dem Klavierauszug überlegte Violinstimme gibt den Urtext wieder

Edition Peters Nr. 4593

11604

4

9

Edition Peters 11604

(Viola)   (Bässe)

11604

RONDEAU
Allegro assai

19